the very best of
AVALON
TESTIFY TO LOVE

2	New Day
12	The Greatest Story
22	Give It Up
30	Everything To Me
42	Testify To Love
51	Adonai
56	Knockin' On Heaven's Door
65	Take You At Your Word
77	Can't Live A Day
84	Always Have, Always Will
93	In Not Of
102	Pray
112	The Glory
118	Wonder Why
127	I Don't Want To Go
134	Don't Save It All For Christmas Day

ISBN 0-634-05973-4

HAL•LEONARD®
CORPORATION
7777 W. BLUEMOUND RD. P.O. BOX 13819 MILWAUKEE, WI 53213

Visit Hal Leonard Online at
www.halleonard.com

NEW DAY

Words and Music by JANNA LONG, JODY McBRAYER,
TEDD TJORNHOM and LYDIA GOTT

Moderately fast

It's a new day. Oh, it's a new time and there's a

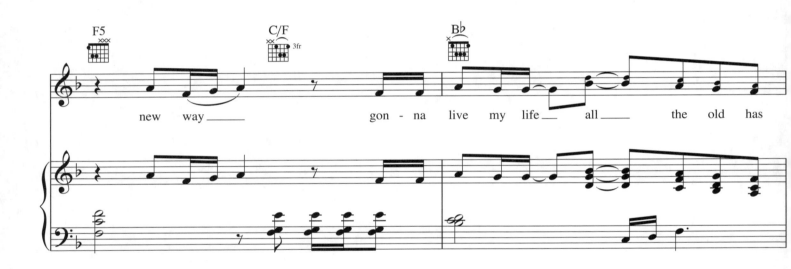

new way gon - na live my life all the old has

passed a - way and the new has come. Thank God, it's a brand new day.

Original key: F# major. This edition has been transposed down one half-step to be more playable.

3

4

passed a-way _____ and the new has _ come. _ (It's a Thank

brand, brand,)
God, _____ it's a brand new _ day. _____ 'Cause of what _ You've done _ for me, _ no,

I am not a-shamed. _ This heart of mine _ is fin - 'ly free; _ I will
(I am not _ a - shamed.) _

nev - er be _ the same, _____
(Nev - er be, _ nev - er be, _ nev - er be _ the same, _

THE GREATEST STORY

Words and Music by DOUGLAS McKELVEY
and CHARLIE PEACOCK

the great-est sto - ry ev - er told.

In the light of e - ter - ni - ty, standing face to face, you will fi - nal - ly see.

For the ver - y first time you'll un - der - stand your

GIVE IT UP

Words and Music by RIKK KITTLEMAN,
MICHAEL PASSONS, GRANT CUNNINGHAM,
MARK HEIMERMANN and JANNA POTTER

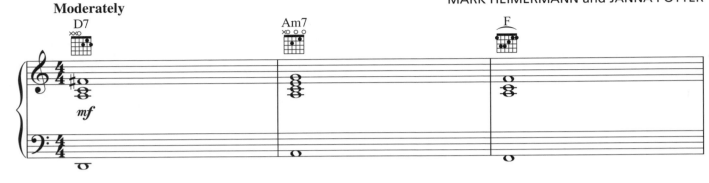

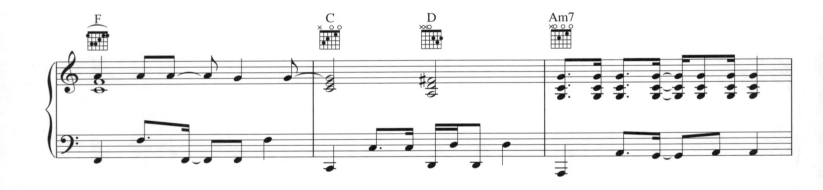

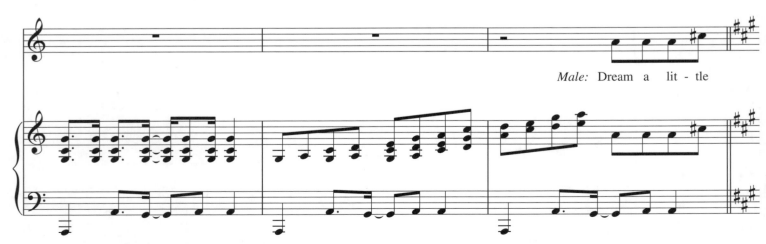

Male: Dream a lit - tle

*Female I lead vocal is written one octave above sounding pitch

EVERYTHING TO ME

Words and Music by CHAD CATES
and SUE SMITH

I want to tell__ the world__ I've found__ a

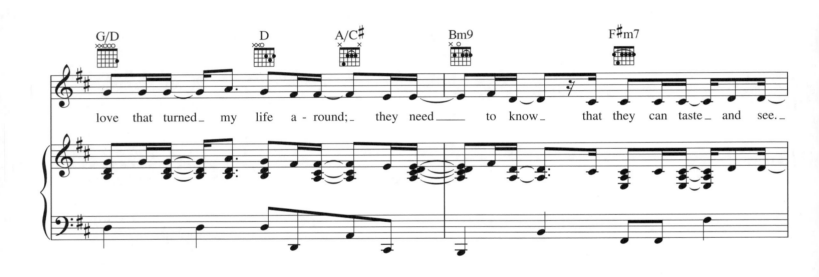

love that turned__ my life a - round;__ they need_____ to know__ that they can taste__ and see.__

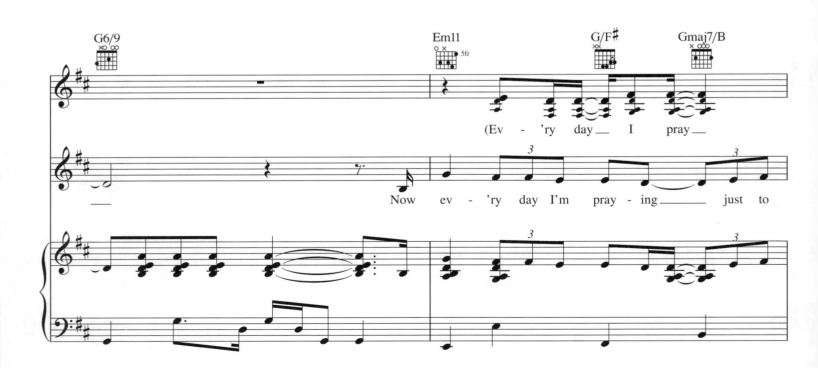

(Ev - 'ry day__ I pray__

Now ev - 'ry day I'm pray - ing_____ just to

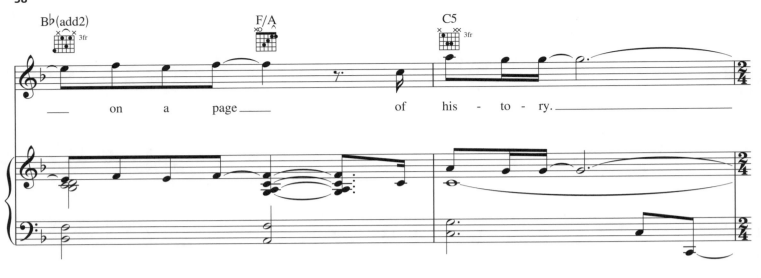

on a page_____ of his - to - ry._____

(Ev - 'ry - thing_____ to me.)_____

Female: You're ev - 'ry - thing to me; You're

(Ev - 'ry - thing_____ to me,

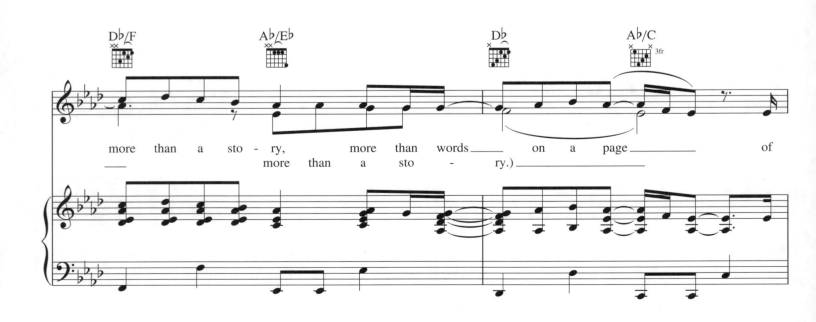

more than a sto - ry, more than words_____ on a page_____ of

_____ more than a sto - ry.)_____

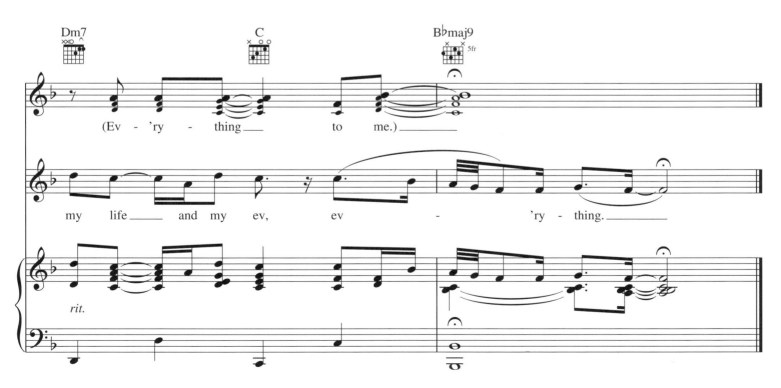

TESTIFY TO LOVE

Words and Music by PAUL FIELD, HENK POOL,
RALPH VAN MANEN and ROBERT RIEKERK

Rhythmically

All the col - ors   of the rain - bow, _
From the moun-tains   to the val - leys, _

46

48

ADONAI

Words and Music by LORRAINE FERRO,
DON KOCH and STEPHANIE LEWIS

54

KNOCKIN' ON HEAVEN'S DOOR

Words and Music by GRANT CUNNINGHAM
and MATT HUESMANN

60

61

TAKE YOU AT YOUR WORD

Words and Music by GRANT CUNNINGHAM
and PAUL FIELD

N

CAN'T LIVE A DAY

Words and Music by TY LACY,
CONNIE HARRINGTON and JOE BECK

80

ALWAYS HAVE, ALWAYS WILL

Words and Music by GRANT CUNNINGHAM,
NICK GONZALES and TOBY McKEEHAN

Part of me __ is the pro-di-gal, part of me __ is the oth-er broth-er.
I was born __ with a way-ward heart; still I live __ with the rest-less spir-it.

(Harmony 2nd time only)

88

IN NOT OF

Words and Music by GRANT CUNNINGHAM
and NICK GONZALES

Come bring the hope _ to hope - less men till the lost _ are found _ in Him.

(Both times)

He came to save the world _ so let us _ be _

To Coda

in and _ not of _____ it. _____

Wait a min - ute, if we say _ we

Share His truth _ with hard - ened hearts. We are not like the world _

We can love it. _____

but we ___ can love it. Come bring the hope _ to hope - less

men till the lost ___ are found _ in Him. He came to save the world _ so

PRAY

Words and Music by DENNIS MATKOSKY,
KEITH BROWN and MARIA VIDAL

my knees beg-gin' You, please, ev-'ry time I stum - ble. Lord, I pray

(Help me, Lord, to find my way back.)

(pray), help me find a way (way). You sac-

-ri-ficed, paid with Your life, gave me the right. Lord, I pray.

THE GLORY
(Of the Blood)

Words and Music by REGIE HAMM
and JIM COOPER

WONDER WHY

Words and Music by GRANT CUNNINGHAM
and MATT HUESMANN

I DON'T WANNA GO

Words and Music by JESS CATES
and YANCY WIDEMAN

Original key: E major. This edition has been transposed down one half-step to be more playable.

DON'T SAVE IT ALL FOR CHRISTMAS DAY

Words and Music by CELINE DION,
PETER ZIZZO and RIC WAKE

Slowly in 1, steadily

* Key of recording: D♭

Don't save it all
(Don't save it all

for Christ - mas

day. Find a way to
day.) (Ooh.)

give a lit-tle love to ev-'ry-one, ev-'ry-where.
(Don't save it

all for Christ - mas
...day. day.) Find

More Contemporary Christian Folios from Hal Leonard

AVALON – OXYGEN

Features all 11 songs from the 2001 release by this dynamic CCM vocal quartet: The Best Thing • By Heart, By Soul • Come and Fill My Heart • The Glory • I Don't Want to Go • Love Remains • Make It Last Forever • Oxygen • Never Givin' Up • Undeniably You • Wonder Why.

_____00306440 Piano/Vocal/Guitar $14.95

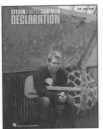

STEVEN CURTIS CHAPMAN – DECLARATION

13 songs: Bring It On • Carry You to Jesus • Declaration of Dependence • God Follower • God Is God • Jesus Is Life • Live Out Loud • Magnificent Obsession • No Greater Love • Savior • See the Glory • This Day • When Love Takes You In.

_____00306453 Piano/Vocal/Guitar $14.95

DC TALK – INTERMISSION: THE GREATEST HITS

17 of DC Talk's best: Between You and Me • Chance • Colored People • Consume Me • Hardway (Remix) • I Wish We'd All Been Ready • In the Light • Jesus Freak • Jesus Is Just Alright • Luv Is a Verb • Mind's Eye • My Will • Say the Words (Now) • Socially Acceptable • SugarCoat It • Supernatural • What If I Stumble.

_____00306414 Piano/Vocal/Guitar $14.95

DELIRIOUS? – GLO

All the songs from the brand new release by these British Christian rockers. Includes: Awaken the Dawn • Everything • God You Are My God • God's Romance • Hang On to You • Intimate Stranger • Investigate • Jesus' Blood • My Glorious • What Would I Have Done? • The Years Go By.

_____00306386 Piano/Vocal/Guitar $14.95

JEFF DEYO – SATURATE

Features 14 powerful tracks, including: All I Want • I Give You My Heart • I'd Rather Have Jesus • Let It Flow • Let Me Burn • Lose Myself • Many Crowns • More Love, More Power • Satisfy • Sing to You • Thank You for Life • You Are Good • You Are Good (Piano & Cello Movement) • You Are Good (Orchestral Movement).

_____00306484 Piano/Vocal/Guitar $14.95

THE KATINAS – LIFESTYLE

Features 14 songs, including their hit "Thank You" and: Beauty of Your Grace • Breathe • Chant • Draw Me Close • Eagle's Wings • I Give You My Heart • I Love You Lord • Live Your Love • Lord, I Lift Your Name on High • Mighty River • Rejoice • Trading My Sorrows • You Are Good.

_____00306485 Piano/Vocal/Guitar $14.95

JENNIFER KNAPP – THE WAY I AM

Includes all 12 tunes from the critically acclaimed CD: Around Me • Breathe on Me • By and By • Charity • Come to Me • Fall Down • In Two (The Lament) • Light of the World • No Regrets • Say Won't You Say • Sing Mary Sing • The Way I Am.

_____00306467 Piano/Vocal/Guitar $14.95

THE MARTINS – GLORIFY/EDIFY/TESTIFY

Features 16 songs: Be Thou My Vision • Gentle Shepherd • Healer of My Heart • In Christ Alone • Jesus, I Am Resting • Lord Most High • Pass Me Not • Redeemed • Settle on My Soul • So High • You Are Holy • more. Includes vocal harmony parts.

_____00306492 Piano/Vocal/Guitar $14.95

BABBIE MASON – NO BETTER PLACE

10 songs from this gospel diva: Change Me Now • Holy Spirit, You Are Welcome Here • The House That Love Built • I Will Be the One • Isn't That Just Like God • Love to the Highest Power • Only God Can Heal • Pray On • Show Some Sign • Stay Up on the Wall.

_____00306357 Piano/Vocal/Guitar $14.95

NICHOLE NORDEMAN – WOVEN & SPUN

Includes all 11 songs from the 2002 release of this Dove Award nominee: Doxology • Even Then • Gratitude • Healed • Holy • I Am • Legacy • Mercies New • My Offering • Never Loved You More • Take Me As I Am.

_____00306494 Piano/Vocal/Guitar $14.95

STACIE ORRICO – GENUINE

This debut release from Orrico features 13 songs: Confidant • Dear Friend • Don't Look at Me • Everything • Genuine • Holdin' On • O.O Baby • Restore My Soul • Ride • So Pray • Stay True • With a Little Faith • Without Love.

_____00306417 Piano/Vocal/Guitar $14.95

THE BEST OF OUT OF EDEN

A great compilation of 13 hit songs: Come and Take My Hand • A Friend • Get to Heaven • Greater Love • If You Really Knew Me • Lookin' for Love • More Than You Know • River • Show Me • There Is a Love • and more.

_____00306381 Piano/Vocal/Guitar $14.95

TWILA PARIS – GREATEST HITS

This folio celebrates Twila's career with 18 hits: Destiny • Faithful Friend • God Is in Control • He Is Exalted • How Beautiful • Lamb of God • Run to You • The Time Is Now • We Bow Down • We Will Glorify • and more.

_____00306449 Piano/Vocal/Guitar $14.95

PHILLIPS, CRAIG AND DEAN – LET MY WORDS BE FEW

This 10-song collection includes: Come, Now Is the Time to Worship • How Great You Are • Let Everything That Has Breath • Let My Words Be Few • Open the Eyes of My Heart • You Are My King • Your Grace Still Amazes Me • and more.

_____00306437 Piano/Vocal/Guitar $14.95

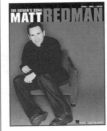

MATT REDMAN – THE FATHER'S SONG

Features 14 songs: The Father's Song • Holy Moment • Justice and Mercy • King of This Heart • Let My Words Be Few • Light of the World • Nothing Is Too Much • O Sacred King • Revelation • Take the World but Give Me Jesus • You Must Increase • more.

_____00306378 Piano/Vocal/Guitar $14.95

REBECCA ST. JAMES – WORSHIP GOD

Includes 12 worship tunes: Above All • Better Is One Day • Breathe • God of Wonders • It Is Well with My Soul • Lamb of God • Let My Words Be Few • More Than the Watchmen • Omega (Remix) • Quiet You with My Love • Song of Love • You.

_____00306473 Piano/Vocal/Guitar $14.95

ZOEGIRL

11 terrific songs from this debut album: Anything Is Possible • Constantly • Give Me One Reason • I Believe • Little Did I Know • Live Life • Living for You • No You • Stop Right There • Suddenly • Upside Down.

_____00306455 Piano/Vocal/Guitar $14.95

FOR MORE INFORMATION, SEE YOUR LOCAL MUSIC DEALER, OR WRITE TO:

HAL•LEONARD® CORPORATION

7777 W. BLUEMOUND RD. P.O. BOX 13819 MILWAUKEE, WI 53213

For a complete listing of the products we have available, Visit Hal Leonard online at
www.halleonard.com

Prices, contents and availability subject to change without notice.

0203